How to Deal with
ASTHMA

W9-CES-541

Lynette Robbins

PowerKiDS press.

New York

For Al

Published in 2010 by The Rosen Publishing Group, Inc.
29 East 21st Street, New York, NY 10010

First Edition

Editor: Joanne Randolph
Book Design: Kate Laczynski
Photo Researcher: Jessica Gerweck

Photo Credits: Cover, pp. 1, 14 Gary Ombler/Getty Images; p. 4 © www.istockphoto.com/wsphotos; p. 6 3DClinic/Getty Images; p. 8 © Jim Craigmyle/Corbis; p. 10 Petri Artturi Asikainen/Getty Images; p. 12 © Picture Partners/Age Fotostock; p. 16 © Roy Morsch/Corbis; p. 18 © Michael Keller/Corbis; p. 20 Shutterstock.com.

Library of Congress Cataloging-in-Publication Data

Robbins, Lynette.
  How to deal with asthma / Lynette Robbins. — 1st ed.
    p. cm. — (Kids' health)
  Includes index.
  ISBN 978-1-4042-8141-7 (lib. bdg.) — ISBN 978-1-4358-3418-7 (pbk.) —
ISBN 978-1-4358-3419-4 (6-pack)
  1. Asthma in children—Juvenile literature. I. Title.
  RJ436.A8R63 2010
  618.92'238—dc22
                                    2009007653

Manufactured in the United States of America

CONTENTS

Asthma Attack!

Luke was playing basketball with his friends at recess. He was about to shoot the ball when he felt a tightness in his chest. He felt as if he could not get enough air into his **lungs**. He started to take quick, short breaths. Then he started to cough. Luke has asthma. He was having an asthma attack.

People who have asthma are fine most of the time. However, sometimes they have trouble breathing. That can be very scary. People who have asthma can take **medicine** to help them feel better. Luke used his medicine to help him begin breathing normally again.

This boy had an asthma attack while playing soccer. If you have a plan in place for how to handle an attack, you can make yourself feel better fast.

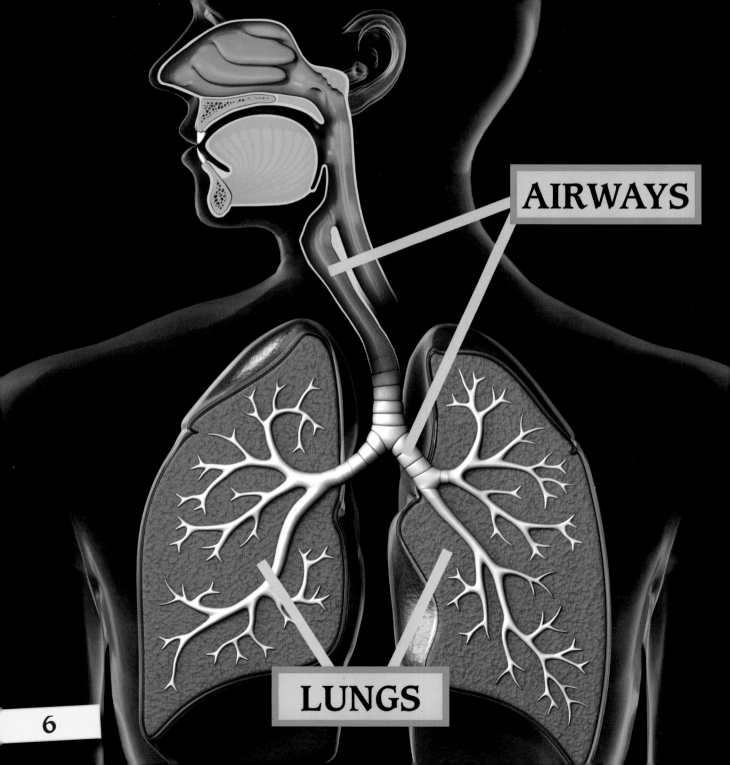

AIRWAYS

LUNGS

What Is Asthma?

Asthma is an illness that makes it hard for people to breathe. Most people who have asthma have it for their whole lives.

Every time you take a breath, you bring air into your lungs. The air comes through your nose or mouth and travels through tubes called **airways**. When a person has an asthma attack, the airways get swollen and **inflamed**. That makes the openings in the breathing tubes smaller, which makes it harder for air to go through them. The airways may also fill with **mucus**. The mucus makes it even harder for the person to get air to her lungs.

This picture shows the lungs and the airways, or the tubes that carry air throughout the lungs. These tubes get smaller when a person has an asthma attack.

The First Attack

Mia remembers her first asthma attack. She was just four years old. She was playing outside when she started to have trouble breathing. She felt as if a full-grown person were sitting on her chest.

Like Mia, a person who is having an asthma attack has trouble breathing. He may take short, quick breaths to try to get enough air into the lungs. The person's breath may make a whistling sound. This is called **wheezing**. This sound is caused by air trying to move in and out of the inflamed airways that cause an asthma attack. He may cough. The person may also have a tight feeling in his chest. If you have asthma, you may remember your first attack, too.

If you have an asthma attack, your parents will likely take you to the doctor. This girl is explaining to her doctor what happened and how it felt when she had her attack.

What Brings It On?

Most people who have asthma feel fine until something **triggers** an asthma attack. Different people have different triggers. Getting sick is a common trigger. When a person who has asthma gets a cold or the flu, she may also get asthma attacks.

Cigarette smoke, air **pollution**, and other strong smells, such as gasoline or perfume, can trigger asthma attacks. Just breathing cold air triggers an attack for some people. Crying, laughing, or getting very angry can also cause an attack. Some people get asthma attacks when they are very active. Running fast or playing sports can cause an attack for these people.

These girls are picking and smelling wildflowers. For someone with asthma, smelling a flower could trigger an asthma attack.

Asthma and Allergies

Emma has **allergies** and asthma. Emma is allergic to cats. When Emma gets near a cat, she has an allergic reaction to the cat. This triggers an asthma attack.

Many people who have asthma also have allergies. People who have allergies have a bad reaction to things like **pollen**, **dust mites**, some animals, and certain foods. When people have allergic reactions, they may sneeze and get watery eyes, a runny nose, or a rash. Often an allergic reaction will also trigger an asthma attack in these people. People with allergies and asthma must stay away from the things to which they are allergic.

People with asthma have to be extra careful to stay away from things to which they are allergic. A runny nose could quickly turn into an asthma attack for these people!

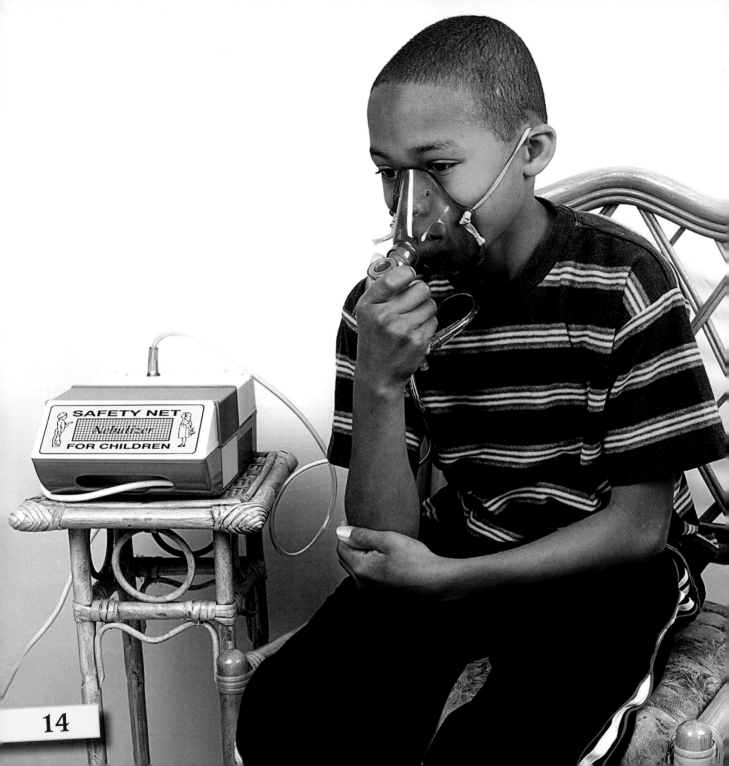

SAFETY NET
Nebulizer
FOR CHILDREN

14

How Bad Is It?

Most people who have asthma have mild asthma. They do not get attacks very often. When they do get an attack, it is not very bad. People with mild asthma can use medicine to start breathing normally again.

Some people have **severe** asthma. People with severe asthma have more asthma attacks. The attacks may also be much more **serious**. A person who is having a severe asthma attack may not be able to talk or walk. This person's medicine may not be enough to stop the attack. A person who is having a severe attack may need to be rushed to a hospital for treatment.

This boy is using a machine called a nebulizer to open his airway during a bad asthma attack. A nebulizer puts medicine into a mist that he breathes in through the mask.

Taking Your Medicine

People who have asthma take medicine for it. Some kinds of medicine are taken every day. They help keep asthma attacks from happening. They work to keep lungs from becoming inflamed. People who have asthma and allergies may need to take daily allergy medicine, too.

Another kind of medicine is taken when a person is having an asthma attack. Most people who have asthma carry this medicine with them wherever they go. The medicine comes in the form of an **inhaler**. The inhaler sends the medicine right to the lungs. The medicine helps open up the airways so that the person can breathe again. Most people breathe better very quickly when they use their inhalers.

This boy uses his inhaler to stop an asthma attack quickly. If you use your inhaler many times a week, talk with your doctor to make sure your daily medicine is working.

Have a Plan!

Do you have asthma? Then you need to be prepared! Always make sure your inhaler is nearby. Teach your babysitters, teachers, and other adults who take care of you about your asthma so they can help you if needed.

Be aware of how an asthma attack starts for you. Some people have trouble breathing. Others may just feel a little tired or overheated. Those early signs may be warning you that an asthma attack is about to happen!

If you feel an asthma attack coming, stop what you are doing. Stay calm. Tell an adult right away. Then use your inhaler. Rest quietly until you feel better.

A doctor can help you and a parent come up with a plan to control your asthma. She can teach you when and how to use your inhaler and why it is important to act quickly.

20

Get in the Game!

Do you like to play sports? Most people enjoy playing sports and being active. Being active is good for you, too! It keeps your body and your lungs strong. Some people's asthma is triggered by exercise. Should they stop exercising? No! Exercise is good for people with asthma, even those who are more likely to have attacks during exercise. These people need to be careful, though. They should work with their doctor to come up with a plan to stay active without triggering an attack.

People who have asthma need to listen to their bodies and take care not to play too hard. They may need to rest more than people who do not have asthma.

By being careful, people with asthma can have fun playing sports and make their lungs stronger, too! This girl with asthma swims on the swim team every year.

If you take good care of yourself and your body, asthma does not have to stop you from having fun. The best way to take care of yourself is to stay away from things that trigger your asthma. It is also important to always keep your inhaler nearby and use it as soon as you feel an attack coming.

Staying active can help, too. Whenever you exercise, you make your lungs stronger! That means fewer asthma attacks. Asthma attacks are not fun, but most of them do not last very long. Stay calm and follow your plan if you have an attack. Soon, you can go back to having fun again!

GLOSSARY

airways (EHR-wayz) Tunnels for air that tie the nose or mouth to the lungs.

allergies (A-lur-jeez) Bad reactions to certain things, such as animals or pollen.

dust mites (DUST MYTS) Tiny eight-legged animals whose droppings cause allergic reactions in some people.

inflamed (in-FLAYMD) Sore or swollen.

inhaler (in-HAY-ler) Something that helps people with asthma breathe in medicine.

lungs (LUNGZ) The parts of a person that take in air and supply oxygen to the blood.

medicine (MEH-duh-sin) A drug that a doctor gives you to help fight illness.

mucus (MYOO-kus) A thick, slimy matter produced by one's body.

pollen (PAH-lin) A powder made by the male parts of flowers.

pollution (puh-LOO-shun) Humanmade waste that hurts Earth's air, land, or water.

serious (SEER-ee-us) Having to do with something weighty or important.

severe (suh-VEER) Very bad.

triggers (TRIH-gerz) Something that causes something else to happen.

wheezing (WEEZ-ing) Whistling sounds made by a person or animal that is having trouble breathing.

INDEX

WEB SITES

Due to the changing nature of Internet links, PowerKids Press has developed an online list of Web sites related to the subject of this book. This site is updated regularly. Please use this link to access the list: www.powerkidslinks.com/heal/asthma/